LIFE ON A GIANT CACTUS

The saguaro is a giant cactus so beautifully suited to life in the Sonoran Desert of Arizona and Mexico that it can live nowhere else. In fascinating detail the author traces the life history of this big cactus, which may reach a height of 50 feet during a life that spans two centuries, and explains how and why it thrives in the world of the desert. She then describes how desert animals find food in the flowers, fruits, and seeds of the saguaro and shelter in its trunk and branches. And she explains how, in filling their own needs, the animals fill certain needs of the saguaro. The giant cactus is truly a little world within the desert world.

LIFE ON A GIANT
cactus

By Patricia Lauber

GARRARD PUBLISHING COMPANY
CHAMPAIGN, ILLINOIS

Photo Credits

Jen and Des Bartlett from Bruce Coleman: pp. 25, 36, 56, 57
Harold Coss: pp. 13 (top), 21, 41, 44, 48 (all), 49 (all), 50, 61
Allan D. Cruickshank from National Audubon Society: p. 54 (all)
Dave Davis from Davon: pp. 2, 10
Bruce Hayward: p. 34
Ross E. Hutchins: p. 39 (bottom)
Earl King from Davon: pp. 13 (bottom), 63
Lanks from Monkmeyer: p. 6
Mervin W. Larson: p. 38
Karl H. Maslowski from National Audubon Society: p. 52
Bucky and Avis Reeves from National Audubon Society: p. 19
Shostal Associates: p. 12
U.S. Department of Agriculture photo by George Olin: p. 31
Joseph Van Wormer from National Audubon Society: p. 39 (top)
Lewis W. Walker from National Audubon Society: pp. 55, 59
Jeanne White from National Audubon Society: p. 26

Cover Photograph

by Jen and Des Bartlett from Bruce Coleman

Library of Congress Cataloging in Publication Data

Lauber, Patricia.
Life on a giant cactus.

(Good earth)
SUMMARY: Describes the life cycle of the giant
cactus, the saguaro, which grows only in the Sonoran
Desert of Arizona and Mexico.
1. Saguaro—Juvenile literature. 2. Desert ecology—
Sonoran Desert—Juvenile literature. 3. Sonoran
Desert—Juvenile literature. [1. Saguaro. 2. Cactus.
3. Desert ecology]   I. Title.
QK495.C115L38   583'.47   74–4479
ISBN 0–8116–6101–6

CONTENTS

1. A DESERT GIANT

The plant stands 50 feet tall. It has six big branches that curve toward the sky. It is green and covered with sharp spines. It is about 200 years old.

Among its branches is a large, ragged nest. This belongs to a red-tailed hawk. Smaller birds nest inside the plant. Insects and spiders live in it. Bats may roost in it. The plant's flowers, fruits, and seeds provide food for many animals.

What is this plant?

It is a giant cactus, the kind named saguaro.* There are bigger cactuses in

*Pronounced suh - WAH - ro or suh - GWAH - ro

Mexico and South America. But north of Mexico, the saguaro is king. It is the biggest cactus.

That is why it is one of the best-known cactuses. If you are near a saguaro, you cannot help seeing it. It is so big that it makes everything else look small. It is the cactus most people think of when they hear the word *desert*.

Yet the saguaro is not found in every desert. It grows in only one—the Sonoran Desert of Arizona and Mexico.

Like all deserts, the Sonoran is a dry land. It is a place where little rain falls.

Months go by with no rain. Springtime is dry. Early summer is dry. Each day the air is clear and warm. The sky above is blue.

Rain does not come until the middle of summer. Then it falls in violent thunderstorms, drumming on the sunbaked land. Some water soaks in, but most of it runs off into gullies. Soon the skies clear and the sun comes out. A day or two later, rain falls again.

By late summer the rains have stopped. Autumn is also dry. So is early winter. Then rain may come again.

Only certain kinds of plants can live in such a place. Each must be somehow suited to life in a dry land. Yet a surprising number are able to live in the Sonoran Desert. There are carpets of spring flowers. There are woody plants, such as mesquite, paloverde, and catclaw. And most of all there are cactuses.

About 50 kinds of cactuses live in the Sonoran Desert. They grow in all shapes and sizes. Some are shaped like barrels; others are like the pipes of an organ, or clumps of sticks, or pincushions. Some cactuses are tiny. Fully grown, a pincushion cactus may be only about 2

A carpet of wild poppies
blooms in early March.

inches high. Some are big—a saguaro towers over its neighbors. Others can be any size in between.

Big or small, all cactuses belong to the same plant family. They are alike in

A prickly pear cactus blooms by this paloverde tree. When water is scarce, the paloverde sheds its leaves. This cuts down the amount of moisture given off.

Organ pipe cactus
grows 20 feet tall.

Pincushion cactus
is only inches high.

many ways. All are desert plants. All can live in a land of little rain. A few kinds can also live outside the desert. But many kinds can live only in deserts.

The saguaro is at home only in the Sonoran Desert. And it is very much at home there. Like its relatives, the giant cactus has ways of living in a dry land. It can take in the water it needs. It can store the water. It can make the water last until the rains finally come again.

2. AT HOME IN THE DESERT

A big saguaro stands as high as a five-story building. It may weigh 8 tons. You might think that this giant's roots must reach deep into the earth. But that is not so. The saguaro's roots are very shallow. They spread out, not down.

A saguaro's taproot goes down 2 or 3 feet. Other roots branch out from the taproot. These are 8 to 20 inches beneath the surface, where they form a huge network. Some are 50 feet long. They reach out all around the saguaro.

The roots both anchor the plant and take in water when rain falls.

A big saguaro is likely to be growing in loose, rocky soil. Rain soaks quickly into such soil. It soon reaches the wide network of shallow roots. They begin to take in water. As they do, something else happens. The touch of water causes the main roots to put out still more roots. These are called rain roots, and they are like very long hairs. While the ground is wet, the rain roots suck up water. When the ground dries, they are no longer needed. They drop off.

In the desert, ground dries fast once the rain has stopped. But by then the saguaro's roots have taken in a large amount of water. During a real downpour, a big saguaro can take in a ton of water.

Water is stored inside the saguaro. Its trunk and branches are filled with soft, pulpy flesh. The flesh holds water much as a sponge does.

A saguaro also has extra storage space. Its trunk and branches are pleated, like the folds in an accordion. As the plant takes in water, the pleats open up. The trunk and branches swell.

By looking at a saguaro, you can tell if there has been a good rainy season. Deep pleats mean that it has been a long time since rain fell. Open pleats mean that there has been rain. The cactus is plump with water.

A tall, plump cactus is holding several

tons of water. Yet the inside of a saguaro is soft flesh. Why don't the branches snap off? Why doesn't the trunk crumple?

The answer is that the saguaro has woody ribs. Inside the trunk is a ring of 12 to 25 wooden rods. These run the length of the trunk and branches. They strengthen the plant. They keep it from breaking, even when it is swollen with tons of water.

This stored water is all the saguaro has until rains fall again. It must last for at least five to six months. If the rains do not come, it may have to last for a year or more. A saguaro needs to hoard its water, to make the supply last. It does this by giving off only a little water to the air.

Flesh of this dead saguaro has rotted away, revealing the wooden rods that strengthened the plant.

All plants must give off some water to the air. They take in water, use it, and give it off. They do this much as we must take in air, use it, and breathe it out. Plants give off water through the surface of their green parts.

Most kinds of plants give off large amounts of water. A big oak tree, for example, gives off about 150 gallons of water a day. The water passes out of the tree through its leaves. An oak tree has thousands and thousands of leaves. Together they have a huge surface area.

A saguaro has a much smaller green surface, for it has no leaves. Its green parts are its trunk and branches. Their surface area is much smaller than the total area of the oak tree's leaves.

Also, the saguaro's trunk and branches have a thick, waxy skin. It seals the water in. The skin has only a few tiny openings where water is given off.

The skin bristles with sharp spines. Each casts a tiny shadow. The many

A young saguaro bristles with sharp spines.

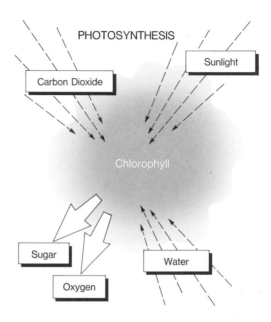

Green plants make their own food by a process called photosynthesis, which means "putting together with light." The process is carried on by the plants' green coloring matter, chlorophyll,

- which uses water from the soil,
- the gas, carbon dioxide, from the air,
- and energy from the sun.

tiny shadows give shade to the skin. They help to cool it. They also break up the flow of hot, dry desert air. The spines cut back the amount of water that is carried away from the cactus.

In the oak tree, each green leaf is a tiny food factory. It makes a kind of sugar that is the tree's food. In the saguaro, this work is done by the trunk and branches. They hold the green coloring matter called chlorophyll that is needed to make food.

In all these ways, the saguaro is suited to life in the desert. It grows where rain sinks quickly into the ground. Its shallow, widespread roots suck up large amounts of water. Its flesh stores the water. And the saguaro has ways of hoarding this water, of not losing it to the dry desert air.

All this is important to the saguaro. It is also important to the animal life of the desert, for animals cannot make food. Among living things, only green plants can make their own food. If there are green plants, then there can be animals. There can be animals that get their food from plants. There can be animals that get their food by eating the plant eaters.

A big saguaro is a source of food in the desert. Many animals find part of their food in the saguaro—in its flowers and fruits, and in its seeds and seedlings. They need the saguaro. And it is also true that the saguaro needs animals.

3. FLOWERS AND FRUITS

In spring, flower buds appear on the saguaro, circling the tips of its trunk and branches. A big saguaro may have 300 buds. Of these, only about a third will open. Some do not get enough

A saguaro flower bud opens into a creamy white blossom that is the state flower of Arizona.

sunlight. Some are attacked by insects that eat them—and by birds that eat the insects.

A saguaro's flowers begin to open in late April or early May. They open at a rate of several a day, and so the blooming spreads over a month. The flowers are creamy white and are surprisingly small for such a big plant. But each is heavily loaded with the yellow grains called pollen. Each is also rich in the sweet, sugary liquid called nectar.

The pollen and nectar draw animal visitors to the flowers. Birds come to drink the nectar. So do bats. Honeybees collect nectar and pollen and carry them back to the hive. Other kinds of

Buds and flowers ring the tips
of the saguaro's trunk and branches.

bees also visit the flowers, as do moths. There is plenty of food for all.

Animals visit the flowers to fill their need for food. But by filling their own need, they do something that helps the saguaro. They carry pollen from one flower to another. As a result, the saguaro flowers are able to produce seeds.

This is what happens. Deep inside each flower are many tiny bodies called ovules. These look like seeds, but they are not. If you planted them, nothing would happen. Yet ovules can become seeds. An ovule becomes a seed if a grain of pollen unites with it. That is, ovules must be fertilized by pollen to become seeds.

INSIDE A FLOWER

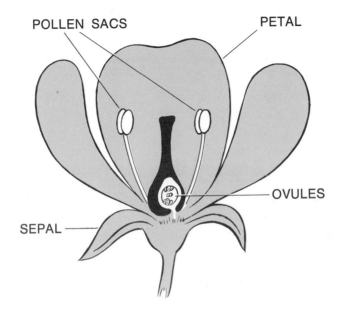

POLLEN SACS

PETAL

OVULES

SEPAL

First, of course, the pollen must reach the ovules.

In some kinds of plants, the pollen does not have far to go. It fertilizes the ovules of its own flower. In many other plants, pollen cannot do this. It can only fertilize the ovules of some other flower. The saguaro is one of these plants.

Saguaro pollen must travel from one flower to some other flower. It must travel quickly. A saguaro flower is open for only a short time. Its petals open one evening, between sunset and midnight. The next afternoon they close. This means that a flower is open for less than 24 hours. The flower can be fertilized only during this period.

What is more, each plant has only a few flowers open at a time. Pollen grains must somehow travel from their flower to a flower on another branch or on another plant.

The pollen travels on the animals that visit the flowers to feed. There are many such visitors, for the flowers are rich in food. Each holds thousands

As this white-winged dove feeds on the nectar of a saguaro flower, its head becomes powdered with pollen.

of pollen grains. Each holds 1/6 of an ounce of nectar, which is about 125 beeloads. The visitors come by day and by night.

The white-winged dove is a day visitor. At the time saguaros start to bloom, flocks of white-winged doves

arrive from Mexico. A dove will perch on a cactus and dip its bill into an open flower. As the dove drinks nectar, its head becomes powdered with pollen. When it flies to another flower, it carries the pollen along. Some rubs off in the next flower.

The honeybee is another day visitor. As it crawls into a flower, grains of pollen stick to its body hairs. When the bee flies off, the pollen goes too.

Sometimes one bee visits the same flower over and over. It makes trip after trip between that flower and the hive. But in the crowded hive it brushes against other bees. They too have pollen in their body hairs. Pollen rubs off one bee onto another. When the bee flies back to its flower, it is carrying pollen from another flower.

The white saguaro flower has a number of night visitors. Among them are the long-nosed bats. Like the doves, these bats arrive in Arizona just as the saguaros start to bloom.

The long-nosed bat is small and brown. It has short, round ears—and a very long nose. Its tongue is also long and covered with bristles. The tongue serves as a long brush, and it is just right for gathering nectar and pollen.

A long-nosed bat may swoop toward a flower and brake in the air. It may feed quickly and fly off without landing on the flower. Or it may grasp the petals and force its small body into

A long-nosed bat pauses in flight to feed from a flower.

the open flower. It is so gentle that it does not harm the flower. Before long, its head is covered with pollen. Some brushes off in the next flower the bat visits.

Still other animals visit the saguaro flowers. Cactus wrens and thrashers dip their bills into the blossoms. So do Gila* woodpeckers and gilded flickers. Moths and different kinds of bees visit the flowers. Another visitor is the hog-nosed bat, a long-tongued relative of the long-nosed bat.

Many different animals may take food from saguaro flowers. Because they do, seeds begin to form.

As seeds form, a change takes place in the flowers. Part of each fertilized

*Pronounced HEE - luh

35

When ripe fruits burst open,
birds, such as this cactus wren,
feed on them.

flower thickens. It becomes a fruit. The fruit protects the seeds.

A fruit ripens about five weeks from the time that the flower opened. On the outside, a saguaro fruit looks like a green fig. The inside is pulpy and bright red. The red flesh is packed with tiny black seeds.

The ripe fruits are eaten by many desert animals. Birds cluster on saguaros to peck at the sweet fruits. Coyotes, ground squirrels, and pack rats gobble fruits that fall to the ground. So do birds and insects.

As the birds and larger animals eat the fruits, they also swallow the seeds. Yet this, too, fills a need for the saguaro.

4. SEEDS AND SEEDLINGS

Like many other seeds, the saguaro's
have a need to travel. They need to
move away from the parent plant.
They need to spread out. A young
plant needs a place of its own, with
room to grow. It needs space to
develop its network of roots.

The pack rat is one of
the animals that swallows seeds
while eating saguaro fruits.

In the plant world, some seeds travel on the wind. Some travel in water. Some travel in the coats of animals. Saguaro seeds are likely to travel in the stomachs of animals that eat the fruits.

The coyote, like the pack rat, swallows seeds along with the fruit and spreads them in its droppings.

This harvester ant carries seeds away to its underground nest. (Seed shown is not from saguaro.)

Suppose a coyote gulps down two or three saguaro fruits. It is also swallowing all the seeds of those fruits. The coyote's stomach uses the fruits as food. But it cannot digest the seeds. These pass through the coyote as waste matter. They are likely to drop unharmed on the ground.

The same thing is true of other animals. A bird feasts on saguaro fruits, then flies off to roost. Saguaro seeds fall to the ground beneath the roost in the bird's droppings.

The number of seeds spread by animals is huge, for the number of seeds produced by saguaros is huge.

On a big saguaro, 60 flowers may set fruit. Each fruit holds some 2,000

40

Saguaros grow best on sheltered slopes with rocky soil. Here they may form forests.

shiny black seeds, the size of pinheads. So one saguaro can produce 120,000 seeds a year—and it may do this for 100 years.

There are places in the desert where saguaros grow very well. They grow so well that they form forests, with fifteen or

twenty saguaros to an acre. One acre of big saguaros produces about two million seeds a year.

Yet of these many, many seeds, only a few get a chance to sprout and grow.

Millions of seeds are carried off by harvester ants. One time a scientist experimented by sprinkling 1,000 saguaro seeds on a plot of ground. Within an hour, harvester ants had carried off every single seed.

The ants gather seeds as food. They store the seeds in their underground nests. The nests are so deep that seeds have no chance to sprout.

Other insects and small creatures also use the seeds as food.

Some seeds escape being carried off or eaten. But not all of these are able to sprout.

To sprout, a seed needs just the right amounts of heat, moisture, and light. For example, temperatures should be in the 70s or 80s. Rain must fall. The seed should be at the surface or in a crack where there is plenty of light.

Rocky soil is a help. It traps moisture. It breaks the force of the wind. And it helps to hide the seed from animals that would eat it.

If all goes well, the seed puts out shoots. These are the start of the roots and trunk. The seed becomes a tiny plant, called a seedling.

A seedling does best if it is growing beneath another plant, such as mesquite or a paloverde. Most likely it is growing from a seed dropped by a bird that roosted there. The tiny seedling needs the shade of this other plant.

These young saguaros
are growing under a paloverde,
which serves as a "nurse" tree.

But being a seedling does not mean that the new plant is safe. Many things can and do happen to it.

A heavy rain may wash a seedling out. Its roots are small and shallow.

Or the rains may not come on time. Then a seedling may die. It is too small to store much water.

The seedling is even more likely to be eaten. Saguaro seedlings are a favored food of pack rats and other desert mice and rats. A scientist once set out 800 seedlings in plots of ground. Six months later only 14 were left. All the others had been eaten. In the months that followed, the 14 were also eaten.

Scientists think that of every 250,000

seedlings, only one may live to become a big saguaro.

Part of the reason is that the young plants grow very slowly. Many years must pass before a saguaro is big enough not to be eaten. Many years must pass before it is able to live through very heavy rains—or no rains.

During a saguaro's first years, you could walk by and never see it. At the age of 2 years, it is only 1/4 inch high.

. At the age of 9 or 10, the plant is 6 inches high. At 15, it is barely 1 foot tall. At 25, it is 3 feet tall. At 50 years, the saguaro stands 6 to 10 feet tall. As yet it has no branches.

By the time a saguaro is 60 or 70,

it has left many dangers behind. And by this time, prickly balls have started to appear on the trunk. These are the buds that grow into branches.

The saguaro may go on growing branches until it reaches its full size. That happens when it is about 150 years old. It is then 35 to 50 feet tall. Its trunk measures about 1 foot across at the base. It is likely to have six or seven branches. And it may live for another 50 or 60 years.

Once in a while, a saguaro appears that is a giant among giants. Such giants are rare. But saguaros are not. Most seeds may be carried off and most seedlings eaten. Still, some of the seeds do sprout and become seedlings.

HOW
SAGUAROS
GROW

1

2

4

3

1. A seed has sprouted; the seedling is two or three days old.
2. A one-year-old saguaro is almost invisible.
3. This one is five years old and still tiny.
4. This two-foot-tall saguaro is eighteen years old.
5. Young saguaros (in front) are about 50 years old.
6. These are the budding branches on a 60- or 70-year-old saguaro.
7. This one is more than 150 years old.

A giant among giants—how many branches does it have? Count the ones you see and multiply by two.

Some seedlings live and grow into big cactuses. In places that are just right, thousands of saguaros cover hundreds of acres. These big cactuses are an important source of food for desert animals. They are also a place to live.

5. AT HOME IN A GIANT CACTUS

For many animals, a giant saguaro is like a hotel in the desert. It is a place to stay. It is a place to live for weeks or months.

At nesting time, many kinds of birds move into saguaros. The red-tailed hawk builds its nest in the highest place around—among the branches of a saguaro. Smaller birds nest inside the big cactus. They use holes that were chopped out by woodpeckers.

Two kinds of woodpeckers live in the Sonoran Desert. They are the

gilded flicker and the Gila woodpecker. Like woodpeckers everywhere, they are often seen chopping away at plants. Usually they are tunneling after insects. But each spring, these birds chop nest holes in saguaros and other big cactuses.

A woodpecker's strong beak breaks through the thick skin of a saguaro. The bird hollows out a hole in the soft flesh of the cactus.

A woodpecker chops its hole several months before nesting time. As the weeks pass, the cactus heals itself inside. A kind of tough scar tissue forms. It seals off the soft pulp of the cactus. By egg-laying time, the hole is a snug, firm nest. The woodpecker does

Red-tailed hawks perch
beside their young
in a ragged nest
built high in a big saguaro.

not carry materials into the hole and build a nest. The hole itself serves as a nest.

The woodpeckers use their nest holes only once. Every spring they chop out new holes.

This Gila woodpecker chops out a nest hole in a saguaro.

The flesh of this saguaro has rotted away, revealing
nest hole made of tough scar tissue.

The old holes are used by many other desert animals.

At least nine other kinds of birds take over the holes and use them for nesting. These are all birds that cannot chop their own holes. Some are owls—screech owls, elf owls, pygmy owls.

A flycatcher leaves the nest hole it has taken over.

The starling is a nest builder that has learned to use holes. It carries a little grass into the hole.

Another is the sparrow hawk, which is a small falcon. The holes are used by flycatchers and kingbirds and purple martins. They are used by English sparrows and starlings.

The holes are dark and inviting, and the inside of a saguaro is a good place to nest. The outside temperature changes greatly between day and night. But inside the saguaro, the temperature stays fairly steady. By day it is cooler than the outside. By night it is warmer.

There is an interesting thing about some of the birds that use these holes. They are kinds that usually build nests. For example, the English sparrow is a nest builder that has learned to use saguaro holes.

By summer birds are ready to leave their nests. Parents and young give up their nest holes and fly off. Now other animals move in.

Brown bats may roost in them all summer.

An elf owl looks out into the night from its hole.

Cactus mice may move in. Sometimes they climb up the cactus spines to reach the holes. Sometimes they gnaw a passageway up to the hole.

Lizards use the holes. Grasshoppers and katydids move in to escape the heat of day. Honeybees may swarm inside the holes. Wasps nest in them.

Flies breed in the holes. There are spiders and many other small creatures.

Even mosquitoes use the holes. They use them for laying eggs. Mosquito eggs must have water if they are to hatch. There is water in some of the holes. It runs in during the heavy rains of summer.

These same pools of water are used by birds. Birds often fly from hole to hole and look in. When they find a hole with water, they drink.

And so the saguaro is many things to many animals of the desert. It is a place to find water. It is a place to live, to breed, to raise young. It is a place to find food—nectar and pollen, fruits and seeds. Its seedlings are food

Wood rats gnawed this passageway up the saguaro.

for some animals. And certain animals that live on the giant cactus are food for other animals. There are, for example, many insects in the holes and pleats of a saguaro. The insects may be eaten by spiders, which are eaten by lizards and birds.

But animals also fill certain needs of the saguaro. They carry pollen from one flower to another. They spread seeds. The woodpeckers that make nest holes also attack insects that are harmful to the saguaro.

In the desert, as everywhere else, all forms of life are linked.

The plant stands 50 feet tall. It has six big branches that curve toward the sky. It is green and covered with sharp spines.

What is it?

It is a saguaro, a giant cactus. It is a plant that can live in the desert. But it is also much more. It is a little world of life within the desert world.

INDEX